Better Together

The ABCs of Building Social Skills and Friendships

By Dr. Melissa Munro Boyd

To Bryanna, Bryan & Bryson, with Love.

May you always be there for each other, as siblings and friends.

The ABCs of Building Social Skills and Friendships

A is for Admitting Mistakes
B is for Being a Good Sport
C is for Cooperating
D is for De-escalate
E is for Empathy
F is for Following Directions
G is for Greeting Others
H is for Helping Others
I is for Intercultural awareness
J is for Joining Groups
K is for Kindness
L is for Listening
M is for Making Eye Contact
N is for Nonverbal Cues
O is for Observing Social Cues
P is for Perspective Taking
Q is for asking Questions
R is for Respecting Personal Space
S is for Sharing
T is for Taking Turns
U is for Using Polite Words
V is for Voice Tone & Volume
W is for Waiting your turn
X is for eXpressing Ideas, Thoughts and Feelings
Y is for Your health
Z is for Zeal

A is for Admitting mistakes

Apologizing for something you said or did.
"I'm sorry I took your pencil."

B is for Be a good sport

Showing kindness even when things don't go your way. "Good game! I'm glad you won!"

C is for Cooperate

Working together to achieve a goal.
"I'm glad we cleaned up together."

D is for De-escalate

Decreasing emotions
or behavior.
"Calming down helps
me think about what
I say and do."

E is for Empathy

Caring about the feelings of another person.
"I'm glad you are feeling better."

F is for Following Directions

Paying attention to details step by step to complete a task. .
"We built the toy correctly by following all the steps."

G is for Greeting others

To welcome someone with a kind word. "Hi! How is your day going?"

H is for Helping others

Doing something kind for another person.
"I'm glad I can help you."

I is for Intercultural awareness

Understanding similarities and
differences between cultures.
"I love both of our dresses!"

J is for Joining groups

Spending time with others to share
interests and build communication skills.
"It's fun getting to know everyone!"

K is for Kindness

Acts of being friendly, generous, and thoughtful. "I love caring for my puppy."

L is for Listen

Paying close attention to what is being said.
"Thank you for listening to how I am feeling."

M is for Making eye contact

Looking at the person
you are talking to.
"I can tell you are paying
attention to me."

N is for
Nonverbal cues

Using eye contact, facial expressions, gestures, and posture to communicate without speaking. "I can tell you do not want to talk right now."

O is for Observing social cues

Paying attention to expressions and body language. "You look very happy!."

P is for Perspective taking

Considering how someone may see, think, or feel differently about a situation. "The number can be a 6 or a 9."

Q is for asking Questions

Communicating to gain more information. "Can you please repeat what you said?"

R is for Respecting personal space

Keeping a safe space (bubble) to help someone feel comfortable. "I won't interrupt your time alone."

S is for Sharing

Giving something to or enjoying something with another person.
"Thank you for sharing the ball."

T is for Turn Taking

Speaking or doing an activity one at a time. "First you can have a turn and then I will go."

U is for Using polite words

Please

Thank You

You're Welcome

Showing manners by using polite words. "I can use polite words when talking to another person."

V is for Voice tone and Volume

How a voice is heard (friendly, funny, upset)
and what a voice level is (loud or soft).
"You are speaking very loudly."

W is for Waiting your turn

Pausing until it is your turn to do or get something. "I am going to wait patiently in line."

X is for eXpressing disagreement

Kindly saying ideas, thoughts, and feelings that may differ from someone else. "We don't agree, but can still be friends."

Y is for Your health

Practicing good habits that keep myself and others healthy. "Washing hands helps me not spread germs."

Z is for Zeal

Being a good friend by showing
enthusiasm and praising others.
"You are doing an awesome job!"

My Favorite Friendship Skills are?

1._____

2._____

3._____

Be Sure to Check Out the Skills for Kids Book Series

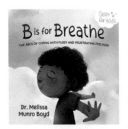    

Instagram.com/author_melissaboyd
Facebook.com/melissamunroboydauthor
www.skillsforkidsbooks.com

19189284R00021